This book belongs to:

____

____

____

Sam was a confident girl who lived in a small city with her Mummy and Daddy. She was friendly and spoke nicely to all of the neighbours while holding Daddy's hand when they went for walks.

All of the people who lived on their road were very friendly and Sam would wave at Mrs. Abeke who looked through the window eagerly as they passed by her house.

3

Mr Patel lived around the corner and Sam would sometimes help him in his garden. She told him what she had learnt at school about plants, sunlight and soil. He smiled as her told her all about his school days in Pakistan whilst he dug up the weeds from the pretty flowerbed.

One evening, Sam noticed smoke coming from Mrs Abeke's house. She ran to the kitchen where Mummy was stirring a large pot of Caribbean soup on the stove.

Sam told her Mummy what she had seen. Mummy wiped her hands on her apron and hurriedly opened the front door. She saw the smoke bellowing from Mrs Abeke's kitchen window and was alarmed.

'Grab my phone please Sam- quickly, quickly!' said Mummy reaching towards her handbag.

Mummy called 999 and within minutes two huge red fire engines rushed onto their road.

The fire fighters sprang into action; they had to break down Mrs Abeke's front door to rescue her and put the fire out with gallons and gallons of water.

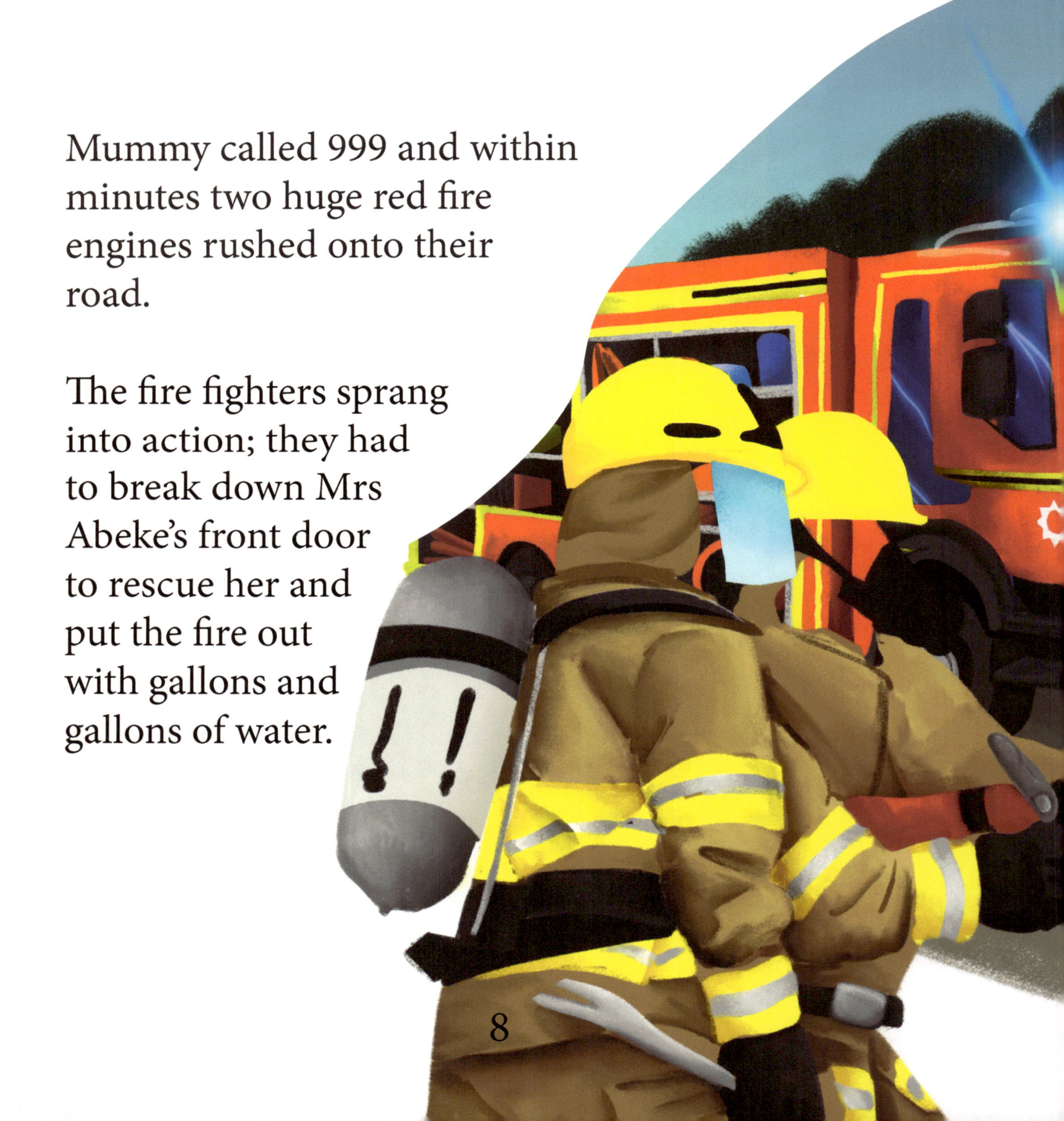

Mrs Abeke was alive, but she could not breathe well. An ambulance with two paramedics arrived at the scene. They put her on a wheelchair and wheeled her into the back of the vehicle while she took deep breaths from an oxygen mask.

Mrs Abeke was unwell for a while but she came home when the repairs to her kitchen were complete. All of the neighbours were happy to see her again!

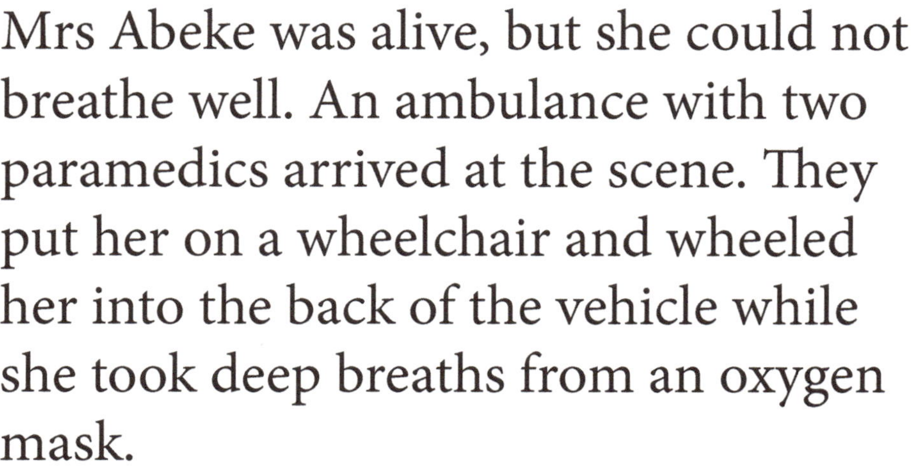

L HEALTH JERVICE
AMBULANCE
NHS
AMBULANCE
11

Sam was invited to the fire station
a few weeks later and was given a
bravery medal because she had done
the right thing and told her Mummy
about the smoke.

The medal was shiny, but a little bit
heavy. She had to hold it with two
hands as she wore it proudly around
her neck!

The fire fighters put a helmet on her
head and helped her climb into the cabin
of the fire engine.

She placed her small hands on the massive
steering wheel and pressed a button that
made the alarm and flashing lights go on
and off.

Sam was so happy to help people like Mrs.
Abeke and decided she wanted to be a fire-
fighter when she grew up.

15

Sam told her teacher about her goal to become a
fire-fighter and he arranged for the whole class to
attend a Fire Safety day as a school trip.

The coach arrived at Sam's school bright and early.
All the children bustled into their seats, put on
their seatbelts and a coach took everyone through
the city streets to the fire station.

Fire-fighter Chang Li met the children and their teachers and took them to a big classroom.

Mr Li helped the children understand the importance of preventing fires, fire alarms, smoke detectors, and fire extinguishers.

He took them into the yard at the back of the fire station, where the huge fire engines were parked.

Sam's Mummy and Daddy were waiting for her when she arrived back from the trip, and she was so excited and happy to tell them about what she had seen!

She told them how Mr Li showed the children long hoses, tall ladders and special tools that were used to cut cars in accidents.

They listened in amazement as told them how she had tried to pick up one of the pieces of equipment, but it was far too heavy for her!

As fire-fighting requires physical strength and endurance,
Sam started to get involved in outdoor activities. She began to play sports, and stay active. She ate all of her meals, drank plenty of water and made sure she went to bed on time.

She also engaged in puzzles, games, and activities that promote problem-solving skills. She realised that Fire-fighters often need to think about danger, and problems. They have to make quick decisions in emergency situations.

23

Sam became more
involved in Community
Service she would go to
the old people's home with
Mommy and talk to the lonely
people there. She would help Mrs
Abeke with her housework and
gardening.

She would ask daddy to place two
or three items in the food bank
receptacle in the supermarkets so
that families who are struggling,
could at least have a warm and
healthy meal

24

BINGO

Sam began to read more books about how to become a fire-fighter. All through secondary school, she worked hard, played well in team sports and listened to her teachers and parents.

She joined the fire-fighter cadets and went to her local station every Tuesday. She learned about the equipment that they use and had the opportunity to try on a big protective suit. It helped to keep them safe from the flames in big fires.

FIRE
CADET
FIRE
CADET
FIRE
CADET

Sam realised that being safe was very important.
She listened to advice from her teachers, church
leaders and parents.

She would examine fire equipment in various
buildings that she visited. I she would identify
the locations of the fire extinguishers and read
instructions on how to evacuate the building in
the event of an emergency.

 She would always be ready to leave the
classroom if there was a fire drill at school
and to follow the fire warden in their bright
fluorescent waistcoat as they took the children
to a place of safety.

She took her national
secondary school
examinations and waited for
the results both times.

She passed her General
Certificate and Advanced
papers in subjects she liked
including geography, music
and English.

31

After Sam had finished
college, she applied to her
local Fire Brigade to become
a fire-fighter. She took
the fitness test and had an
interview for the job.

Due to all the hard work
Sam had done, she passed
the test very easily. The crew
managers were astonished by
how much she already knew
about fire-fighting.

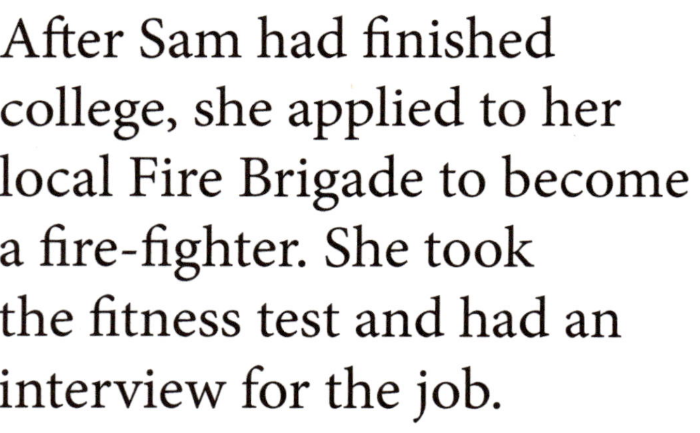

Sam also passed her medical examination where the doctor told her that her heart, lungs, eyes and muscular strength were all sufficient for her to be a good fire-fighter. She had vaccinations that would protect her if she had to go into the water where she could catch diseases like hepatitis.

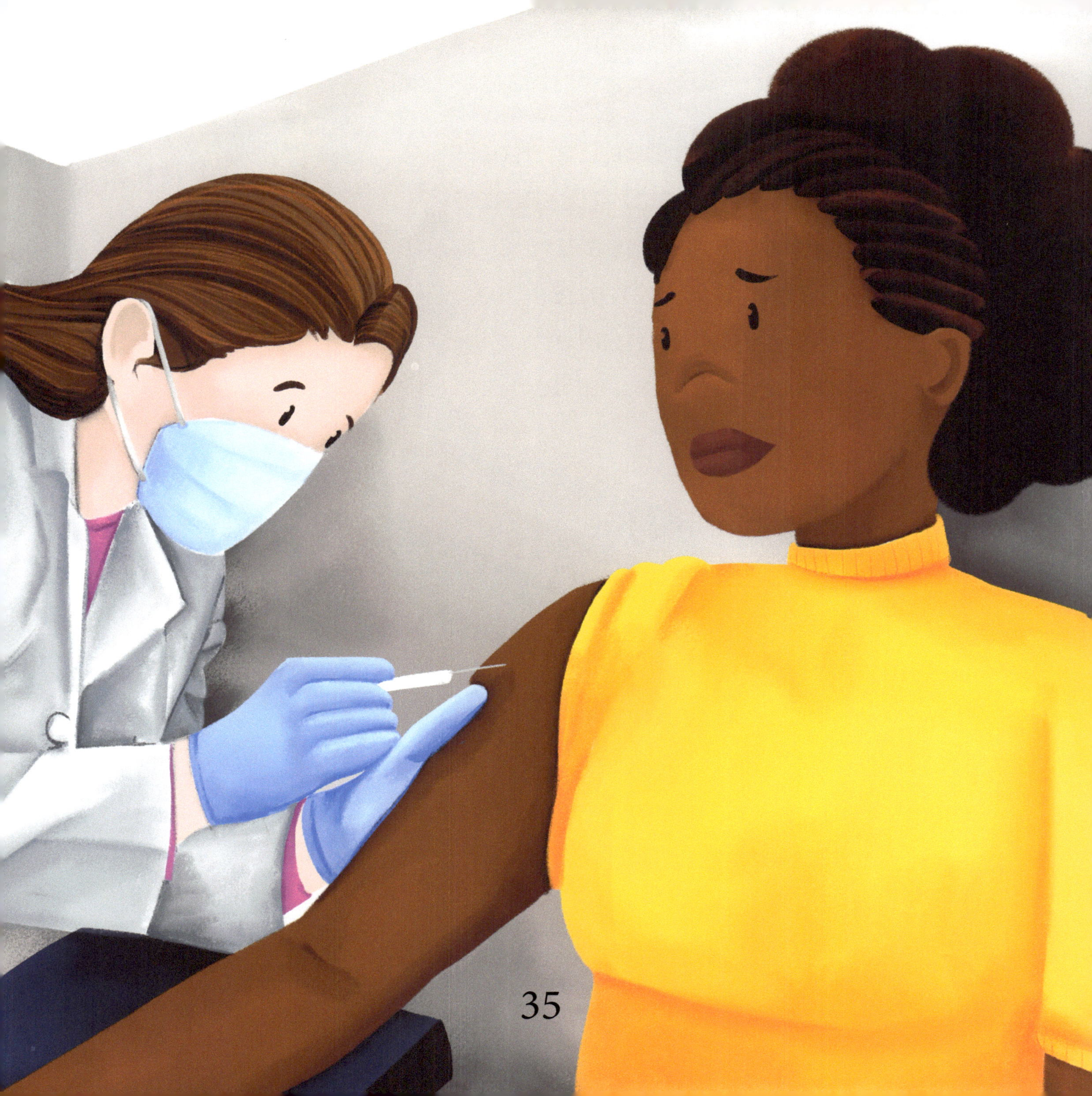

When she finished her training,
she became an official fire-fighter
and joined the team at a fire station,
not too far from her home.
She was always on time for
work and she was a reliable
member of the crew.

All of the staff at the fire
station respected her. They
would listen to her advice
because she was very wise.
The whole crew were successful
in rescuing lots of people from
dangerous situations such as fires,
road traffic accidents or water
incidents.

Sam's crew would enter annual
competitions with a different Brigades
across the country. In these competitions,
the fire-fighters would demonstrate how
quickly they could do their drills and show
how smart and tidy their uniforms were.
Sam was proud of her crew and won some
of the top prizes for three years in a row!

Sam was such a good leader that she
was promoted to crew manager of six
people. After doing this for three whole
years, she became the manager of her
watch, which was an even bigger group
of fire-fighters with
more responsibility!

After working for the Fire Brigade for eight years, Sam became the station commander and she was responsible for all activities in her fire station.

In her new role, Sam was asked to speak in schools to lots of pupils about the importance of being safe and preventing fires. She would also invite the local children to come to the fire station, just as she had done when she was a little girl!

The sparkle of excitement in their eyes reminded her of when she was young.

Sam is now a fearless fire-fighter. She continues to keep herself, fit and healthy and understands ways she can protect people.

She helps the community around her to understand these things as well, so that the young and the old, can stay happy and safe.

If you want to be a fearless fire-fighter, take a look at these references to learn how!

For Kids:

South Wales Fire
Learn how to keep you, your family and friends safe with our interactive games and other learning resources.
https://www.southwales-fire.gov.uk/youth-education/games-and-resources/

London Fire Brigade
Designed for children aged 5-7, learn all about fire safety and what to do in the case of a fire to stay safe.
https://www.london-fire.gov.uk/schools/learning-at-home/fire-safety-education-at-home/

Cartoonio
Fighting Fires - Help Fireman Sam extinguish all the fires!
https://www.cartoonito.co.uk/games/fireman-sam-fighting-fires

Fire Service UK
The UK Fire Service has a dedicated website for the fire service with plenty of details on what is entailed in working in fire and rescue.
https://www.fireservice.co.uk

UCAS
UCAS has a wide range of information on what a firefighters does, what salary you can expect and what career progression is available in the profession.
https://www.ucas.com/careers-advice/how-to-become/firefighter

National Careers
The national careers service has clear guidance on the role of a firefighter and how to enter the profession.
https://nationalcareers.service.gov.uk/job-profiles/firefighter

What do you want to be when you grow up? Draw it below!

Notes!

Check out some other books in the series!

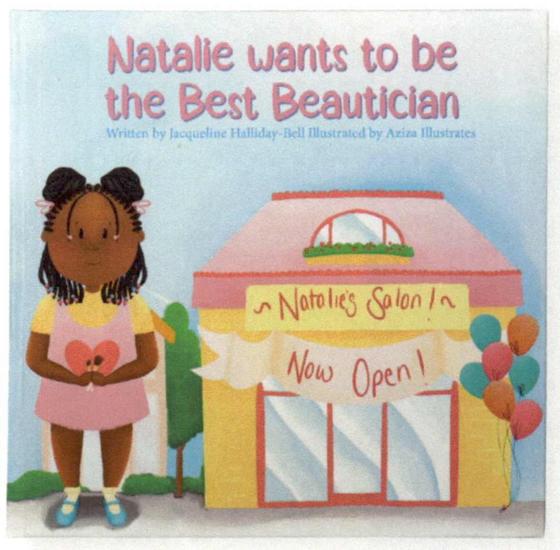